James Brindley
An illustrated life of James Brindley
1716-1772
Harold Bode

Shire Publications Ltd.

Contents

ACKNOWLEDGEMENTS

The author and publishers wish to thank the following for permission to reproduce the illustrations on the pages indicated: Salford Art Galleries and Museums 2; Goose and Sons Ltd. 12 and 24; Radio Times Hulton Picture Library 23 (lower) and 37 (upper); Josiah Wedgwood and Sons Ltd 31 and 34; D.S. Herbert of Southampton 41. The illustrations on pages 16, 27, 29 and 45 are taken from 'Lives of the Engineers, Volume 1' by Samuel Smiles and on page 23 (upper) from the 'Gentleman's Magazine' 1766. The publishers acknowledge with thanks the assistance of R.J. Hutchings of the Waterways Museum, Stoke Bruerne, in the preparation of this book. The photographs on pages 4 (lower), 9, 37 (lower) and 39 are by Michael Johnson (Leek) and the drawing on page 7 is by Robert Cox (Wolverhampton).

The cover photograph by Derek Pratt is Tackley Bridge, Oxfordshire, on the Oxford canal.

Printed by C. I. Thomas & Sons (Haverfordwest) Ltd.

Opposite: James Brindley, anonymous silhouette

Above: Brindley's place of birth at Tunstead near Buxton in Derbyshire. Below: The workshop in Sutton where James Brindley served his apprenticeship to the mill- and wheelwright, Abraham Bennett.

Early life, 1716-1752

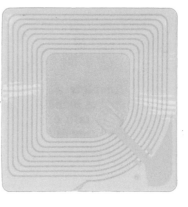

CHILDHOOD AND APPRENTICESHIP

James Brindley was born at Tunstead in the parish of Wormhill about four miles north-east of Buxton, Derbyshire, in 1716. The cottage has long since disappeared but a bronze tablet marks the spot. His father, also James, is said to have been something of a wastrel, but improved himself later, buying a portion in a farm at Lowe Hill, Leek, to which the family moved. Later he purchased the entire property from Richard Bowman of Stockley Hall, near Tutbury. The condition behind the original part sale was that James Brindley, senior, should provide a home at Lowe Hill for his mother, Ellen, Richard Bowman's sister.

Ellen's parents, Henry and Alice Bowman of Alstonfield, were Quakers, who had suffered much, even imprisonment, for their faith. The Quakers, right from the beginning, have been very keen on the education of children. When the Brindleys moved to Leek, the Quaker Meeting House, which would also serve as a school, was already 30 years old, so James Brindley, junior, the future millwright and canal engineer, may have received some schooling there. It is also on record that his mother, Susannah, *née* Bradbury, was a very responsible parent and saw to the education of her children—James, John, Joseph, Henry, Esther, Ann and Mary. James, however, was apparently far more interested in working with his hands, making wooden mills of various kinds and trying them out in wind and stream: he was considered a dull scholar.

In 1733, at the age of seventeen, James was apprenticed to Abraham Bennett, a mill and wheelwright, of Sutton, near Macclesfield, and the workshop, although much modified, still stands, bearing a plaque recording James Brindley's apprenticeship.

Initially he was not too successful. At one time he was left to complete a cart-wheel, but unfortunately, he built it with the spokes leaning in, instead of out, thus ruining it and provoking the wrath of his master, who doubted that he would ever make anything of his apprentice.

However, James Brindley improved. In 1735 he was sent to help in repairing some fire-damaged machinery at a small silk mill in Macclesfield, and the mill foreman was so impressed by his sagacity that he persuaded Bennett to let the apprentice complete the repairs. He did this so satisfactorily that the foreman wagered a gallon of ale that James would be the best of Bennett's workmen by the time his apprenticeship was out. His workmanship was so sound and thorough that on one occasion his master rebuked him: 'Jem, if thou persist in this foolish way of working, there'll be very little trade left to be done when thou comes out of thy time. Thou knows that firmness of wark's the ruin o'trade!'

THE PAPER-MILL AT WILDBOARCLOUGH

Later, Bennett was asked to erect the machinery at a new paper-mill on the Clough brook at Wildboarclough. This was to be on the same pattern as two mills already working at Smedley on the river Irk and at Throstle Nest on the river Irwell near Manchester. Bennett went over to inspect but, on his return, it was quite clear to Brindley that his master had spent more time drinking then studying, having little idea of how to go about the work. So one Saturday night, Brindley walked the twenty-five miles into Manchester. On Sunday morning he sought out the owner of the Smedley Mill, Mr Appleton, and obtained permission to examine the mill. This he did, making notes and storing up the details in his remarkably retentive mind; then he walked back to Macclesfield.

Meanwhile, Bennett, thinking that Brindley, now of legal age, had broken his indentures and gone off, sent to his home in Leek to discover his whereabouts. However, on Monday morning, Bennett found his 'runaway' apprentice busy at work on the paper-mill, and he thereupon handed over the completion of the contract to Brindley, who finished the work to the satisfaction of the owners.

Brindley was later credited with the construction of the automatic water-wheel. This was only scrapped in 1952, no attempt having been made to preserve it. In their heyday Crag

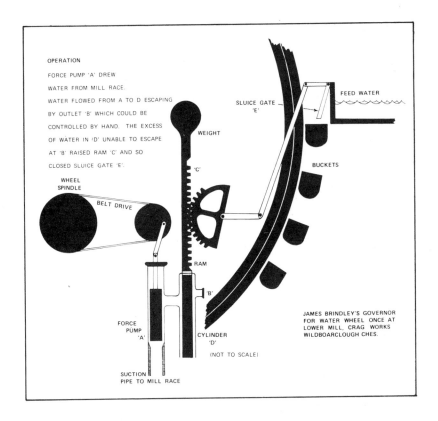

OPERATION

FORCE PUMP 'A' DREW WATER FROM MILL RACE. WATER FLOWED FROM A TO D ESCAPING BY OUTLET 'B' WHICH COULD BE CONTROLLED BY HAND. THE EXCESS OF WATER IN 'D' UNABLE TO ESCAPE AT 'B' RAISED RAM 'C' AND SO CLOSED SLUICE GATE 'E'.

FEED WATER

SLUICE GATE 'E'

WEIGHT

'C'

BUCKETS

WHEEL SPINDLE

BELT DRIVE

RAM

'B'

FORCE PUMP 'A'

CYLINDER 'D'

(NOT TO SCALE)

JAMES BRINDLEY'S GOVERNOR FOR WATER WHEEL ONCE AT LOWER MILL, CRAG WORKS WILDBOARCLOUGH CHES.

SUCTION PIPE TO MILL RACE

Mills at Wildboarclough, having changed over to the manufacture of carpets, employed 647 workers and every week sent twelve wagon-loads of goods to London alone. Now all that remains are the mill dam that supplied the water, the offices (now a post office) and Edinburgh Cottages, named from the Scottish weavers who were brought in to work at the factory.

BRINDLEY MOVES TO LEEK

Abraham Bennett gradually allowed James Brindley to take over the entire running of his business and on Bennett's death, Brindley completed all the work, wound up the business, and moved to set up on his own in Mill Street, Leek, in 1742.

Leek was then a small market town in a poor agricultural area, the only industry, apart from satisfying the needs of agriculture, being the making and dyeing of silk ribbons and threads. The threads were used by the cottagers in the town and in the country around for sewing patterned covers on to wooden buttons. Brindley's prospects were poor, especially as his insistence on good work and quality heightened his prices.

Sometime in the early 1750s, Brindley was asked to rebuild the Leek corn-mill. The situation of the earlier mill is unknown, but as Milne (Mill) Street is recorded for many years prior to 1750, it is safe to assume that it was very close to the present site. Here the river Churnet flows closest to the town, and then makes a loop.

Brindley's pattern of construction may have been as follows. First he cut the mill-race straight across the loop, lining it with massive stones. Then he made the wheel-chamber, 6 feet wide and of blocks of stone. There is a short, curved lead-in of stone to the sill, where the grooves that were cut into the stone to take the original shutter can still be seen. Then the blocks were 'tailored' to match the 16 foot diameter wheel, leaving a 3 inch gap. From the lowest point of the wheel the stones rise to another sill, leading to the tail-race, the first sill being 40 inches higher than the second. It is conjectured that the rise to the second sill was to reduce the chance of back-wash stopping the wheel when the river flooded.

The stonework on each side of the wheel is also recessed in an arc to a depth of about 2 inches, presumably to allow the miller to get down to clear debris from the wheel-pit. The mill side of the chamber supports the north wall of the mill.

Having constructed the race, Brindley directed the river through it by throwing a dam of earth across the entrance to the loop. Behind his dam, the weir was built, first a straight wall, then 23 courses of stones for the top, followed by the face of the weir, 8 courses deep. The rim is an arc, 27 yards round, 5 yards deep. From the straight wall to the arc, the top slopes 1 foot 8 inches, which ensured that water would run off the weir and removed the possibility of damage in freezing weather. The arc shape, of immense strength, would also reduce the speed of flow of the water over the weir, reducing the wear and tear on the structure.

The river banks below the weir were faced with blocks of stone, and the stonework of the weir was tied in with them, giving a very strong structure indeed. Except for wear on the top,

The Brindley Mill and Museum, Mill Street, Leek. The mill was restored and opened to the public in May 1974. It is open to the public on Saturday and Sunday afternoons from Easter to October, also Monday, Tuesday and Thursday afternoons in July and August. At other times by application to the Secretary of the Brindley Mill Trust, K. N. Crawford, 5 Daintry Street, Leek, ST13 5PG.

it is as good over two hundred years later as on the day that it was built.

The river upstream is lined with stone for a hundred yards, and, beyond a modern concrete bridge, is crossed by a small accommodation bridge. Brindley, having increased the depth of the river by the weir and mill-race, had to provide a bridge. This, of stone, has an arch of 25 feet. The stones of the arch are over-laid by flat 'sleepers' of stone that protrude and are a 'Brindley' feature, occurring over and over again in his structures. The bridge is 8 feet wide, with low parapets. Although only designed to serve a meadow, in later years the meadow became the place for all kinds of open-air activities and displays, so the bridge bore the weight of vans, lorries, fire-engines and the like. The bridge is no longer used but it is as sturdy as on the day it was built.

The mill itself is built of a double course of stone, except on the eastern access side, which is of four courses of brick. The walls are pierced by attractive windows with stone frames. The big entrance door has a stone arch with protruding sleepers over, like the bridge.

The water-wheel is 16 feet in diameter and is an 'under-shot' type, in that the drive water passes under it. It is of wood and metal and not original, but then neither the pit-wheel, on the same axle as the water-wheel, nor the 'wallower', the bevel wheel it drives, are original. The perpendicular main shaft is original, however, and is enormous. This carries, on the first floor, the great spur wheel, 9 feet 11 inches in diameter and made of wood with strip teeth bolted on. This is original and drives the pinions of the 'runners' of the three sets of millstones. These pinions have wooden teeth held by wedges. If a tooth broke, its replacement was merely a matter of knocking it out and wedging in another. The sack hoist was driven by another pinion. A stone set into the west wall is inscribed *TI 1752 JB*.

The second floor of the mill was used for storing grain for grinding, and both floors are supported by great oak beams, with six lateral oak beams supporting the roof rafters. They are supported in the middle by a king post structure resting on an arch beam made from a curved oak split in half. The ends rest on the wall and the juncture is held by a metal plate. The oak was carefully selected for this job and would seem to confirm Smiles's statement that in the early days Brindley selected and cut the timber himself.

The bridge, the mill-race, the wheel chamber, the weir and the mill have been described in detail. They are proof that Brindley, as early as 1752, was showing that ingenuity and 'firmness o'wark' that was to bring him fame.

Corn was ground at the mill until 1944. Then it was used as a saw-mill and a garage, although part was demolished shortly after the war. In 1966 a plaque was fixed to commemorate Brindley's connection with it and in 1968 it was scheduled as a building of special historic interest. The Brindley Mill Pre-servation Trust was set up in 1970, the Mill was purchased in 1972 and was opened to the public in May 1974. A museum was created in 1980.

In business

BRINDLEY AT CLIFTON COLLIERY, MANCHESTER

James Brindley's ability to make a success of any job he tackled and his ingenuity in effecting improvements earned him the nickname 'Schemer' and more and more of his work was being done in the developing Potteries area—so much so that in 1750 he rented a workshop in Burslem from the Wedgwoods who had a pottery there. His fame spread further afield, for in the same year he was consulted by John Heathcote about the flooding of the latter's Gal Pit coal mine at Clifton, near Manchester.

This invitation to resolve the problem seems to have come about in this wise:— John Heathcote attended the wedding of his nephew, Michael Heathcote, to Rachel Edensor, both of Hartington, Derbyshire. (Hartington is only about ten miles from Leek.) At some time during the festivities, conversation turned to business, and John Heathcote remarked that his Gal Pit had ceased production owing to flooding. The best means of lifting water at that date was by pony or horse pulling up an oversize bucket or water-barrel by means of a gin, and this had proved inadequate. Brindley's name and reputation were mentioned, a meeting arranged, and Heathcote was so impressed by Brindley's confidence that he agreed to let him find a solution. The fact that work on the scheme did not start until 1752 proves that it was no rushed job; the project was very carefully prepared. The proposals were so unique that John Heathcote must have had complete confidence in Brindley's ability to see them through.

Permission was granted to go ahead, and work started. One wonders now whether it would have started had Heathcote known that it would be 1756, after four years' labour and seemingly endless cost, before it would operate and its success or failure be known. Brindley's scheme was to use the river

HYDRAULIC POWER SCHEME AT CLIFTON

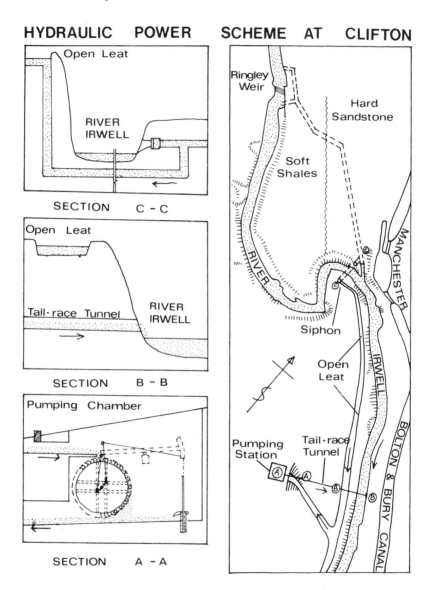

Based on a drawing by Dr C.T.G. Boucher which appeared in 'James Brindley', Goose and Son Ltd. (1968). By permission.

Irwell to draw water from the bottom of the Gal Pit's 158 foot deep shaft.

The pit was near the south bank of the river. Between the pit and the hamlet of Ringley Fold to the west the river Irwell sweeps in a tremendous loop almost half a mile across. Brindley decided to raise the level of the river and control its flow by means of a weir at Ringley Fold. From the north side of the weir, he drove a tunnel approximately 600 yards long across the loop of land. At first it was driven through shale and lined with brick. Then, at the Pendleton Fault, a fracture in the earth's crust that causes mild earth tremors in the area, the tunnel entered sandstone and was unlined. Below the weir a wash-out tunnel was dug from the river bank to the main tunnel for cleaning purposes.

Where the main tunnel reaches the river bank at the eastern end of the loop a vertical shaft was dug to a depth of 53 feet, as well as another wash-out tunnel to the river bank. From the vertical shaft a horizontal tunnel, 220 feet long, was dug under the river bed to another vertical shaft dug down from the south side of the river. The two shafts and the tunnel under the river thus formed an inverted siphon.

From the top of the southern shaft an open leat, or channel, was excavated to a point near the Gal Pit, where it turned south. It entered the hillside by means of another tunnel and here an underground chamber was excavated. In this Brindley installed a water-wheel, some 30 feet in diameter. The water from the weir passed over—over-shot—the wheel which moved the levers to operate the pumps draining the pit.

So the water from the weir at Ringley Fold followed the underground tunnel for 600 yards, passed under the river Irwell by means of the inverted siphon and rose into the leat. This conveyed it to the pumping-chamber where it turned the water-wheel, that worked the pumps and lifted the water out of the mine. To remove the drive and drain water, a tail-race tunnel was dug to the river Irwell.

Only hand tools such as hammers and chisels were available, with candles and tallow dips for illumination. Furthermore, the work space was so constricted that only a handful of men could work. After four years arduous labour, the scheme was complete, the water flowed, the wheel turned, the pumps drained the mine and the production of coal restarted.

Brindley's wheel lasted until 1867, 111 years, when it was replaced by a water turbine. This worked until 1924 when a steam pump took its place. The coal mine was worked from 1756 to 1928 when the colliery closed. Brindley's tunnel, siphon and leat continued to supply industry with water until 1960 when the tunnel site was used for the Ringley Fold Sewage Treatment Works. Even today, the water impounded by Ringley Weir supplies cooling water for the Central Electricity Generating Board's giant Kearsley power station.

The drop in water from the top of the weir to the wheel in the underground chamber was 35 feet, lifting water from a depth of 158 feet, and Brindley became known as the 'man who made water run uphill'. For his labours he received 2s 0d per day; the income from the revived pit is believed to have reached £6,200 per year, giving employment to around 150 persons.

At Clifton, Brindley proved himself to be the leading engineer of his day and perhaps the first 'civil engineer', able to conceive, plan and put through to a successful conclusion a major project, training others to go on with the work while he dealt with projects elsewhere.

His achievement did not go unnoticed for a few miles to the south of Clifton stands Worsley Old Hall, the seat of Francis Egerton (1736-1803), third Duke of Bridgewater, destined to become famous as 'the Canal Duke'.

STEAM ENGINES AND FLINT MILLS

James Brindley's business began to prosper. In 1752 he built the corn-mill at Leek, as well as starting the Clifton Colliery ydraulic scheme. In 1755 he was at work on corn-mills at heelock, Codan, Ashbourne, Marchant Brooks and Trentham, d at Congleton he fitted out a new silk mill.

n 1756 Brindley visited Bedworth, Birmingham and verhampton to study Newcomen's atmospheric steam 1es. (The first practical steam engine had been erected by Newcomen at Dudley, Worcestershire, in 1712 for the purpose of draining a mine.) Brindley then constructed one at Little Fenton, Staffordshire, for Thomas Broad. The enormous cylinder for this was 60 inches in diameter and 10 feet high. He was also busy at this time with water-driven mills at Abbey Hulton and Bucknall, Stoke-on-Trent, and at Congleton.

In 1757 he built a flint mill at Tunstall, Staffordshire, for

Thomas Baddeley. The use of ground flint with clay in making pottery is credited to a William Astbury of Shelton, Stoke-on-Trent. On a journey to London his horse's eyes became inflamed and he asked an ostler for advice. The latter took a piece of black flint-stone, burnt it in the fire and produced a white powder that he mixed with water to poultice the horse's eyes. The potter was so impressed by this that he brought some flintstones home, burnt them to a powder, mixed them with pipe clay and produced the first white stone ware.

The process of reducing flints to powder by hammer and handgrinding was slow, laborious and injurious to health. At Baddeley's mill Brindley built a water-wheel that drove stampers to pound the flints to powder. The wheel also drove the pumps to drain a coal mine some 200 yards away. This was done by means of a crank on the water-wheel moving slide-rods that operated the pumps. This worked successfully for fifty years, but the stampers were superseded by the process described below.

In 1758 Brindley constructed a windmill at a part of Burslem called The Jenkins for Messrs J and T Wedgwood. This was for flint grinding, but here the power was used to drive paddles round a circular vat. The bed of the vat was covered with blocks of Derbyshire chert stone, and large, flat blocks of the same stone were pushed round the vat by the paddles. The burnt flints were placed in front of these stones, the vat filled to the required depth with water, and the end product was a liquid containing ground flint that could be reduced by heating to a powder for use elsewhere, or mixed with the clay for pot manufacture on the spot. Not only did this system meet the ever-growing demand for ground flint, but it removed the hardship and danger associated with the stamping and hand-grinding methods. There is a story that the sails and gearing that Brindley constructed for this mill were so enormous that, on the first day of operation, a gale blew the sails off! This was quickly put right and the mill was a complete success.

Brindley built many flint-grinding mills and one still survives in full working order at Cheddleton, near Leek, having been restored by the Cheddleton Flint Mill Trust.

It was at about this time that Brindley became intimate with a Mary Bennett of Burslem. On 31st August 1760 their son, John Bennett, was baptised; he was the great-great-grandfather of Arnold Bennett (1867-1931), the novelist.

1758 was a busy year for James Brindley. Having satisfactorily restored some water-pumps for Earl Gower at Trentham, he was invited by the Earl and Lord Anson to make a survey for a canal from the Trent to the Mersey. This was not a new idea, for in 1755 the Corporation of Liverpool had had such a survey made. Brindley's survey confirmed the Liverpool one—it could be done, but at a cost beyond his sponsors' means.

Francis Egerton, third Duke of Bridgewater, by T.D. Scott. The Barton Aqueduct is shown in the background.

The Bridgewater Canal

THE YOUNG DUKE

Francis Egerton, later to become the third Duke of Bridgewater, was born in 1736. His father was Scroop, fourth Earl of Bridgewater, created first Duke of Bridgewater in 1720, who had married as his second wife Lady Rachel Russell, sister to the third Duke of Bedford. There were eight children by this marriage, but consumption took its toll. Charles, the eldest, died at the age of six; John, who became second Duke of Bridgewater, died in 1748 aged twenty-one; William and Thomas died in infancy. As the two sons of the first marriage had also died, this left Francis, a frail, sickly child, to become third Duke of Bridgewater and to succeed to the vast estates, including Worsley, near Manchester, and its coal mines. The three daughters lived to a riper age: Louisa, the one who is connected with this story, was born in 1723 and married Granville Leveson Gower, Viscount Trentham, later Earl Gower and Marquis of Stafford.

After the death of Scroop, first Duke of Bridgewater, his widow married Sir Richard Lyttleton. They were too fond of gay society to trouble much about Francis. In fact he was so weak and mentally backward through long illness, that his mother and stepfather thought he would follow his brothers to an early grave, and when John, his eldest brother, died, his mother tried to get Francis's right to the Bridgewater titles and estates set aside. She failed, and Francis was put under the guardianship of John Egerton, John, fourth Duke of Bedford, and Earl Gower.

In 1749 these guardians sent Francis to Eton where he made so much progress in education and health that, in 1752, his guardians decided that he could withstand the rigours of the Grand Tour of Europe and secured the services of Robert Wood as mentor and tutor.

Of the whole Grand Tour, the visit to the Languedoc Canal in France was to have the most lasting effect. The Languedoc Canal, 150 miles long, with the river Garonne, links the Atlantic at Bordeaux with the Mediterranean at Sète. Francis was most impressed for, although tidying rivers to make them more suitable for navigation was not unknown in England, most of the Languedoc Canal was arterial, that is, independent of rivers.

After going on to Italy, Francis was taken seriously ill in Rome and in the autumn of 1755 returned to England. Here he began the gay life of a typical aristocrat about town, drinking, gambling, and buying a racing stable at Newmarket.

Then came the event that brought a dramatic turn to his life. In 1751 Bridget, Countess of Mayo, came to London to bring her beautiful daughters out into the world of fashion. Maria married the Earl of Coventry and Elizabeth married the Duke of Hamilton whose dissolute way of life soon led to his demise.

Francis met this young, beautiful, rich, widowed duchess and promptly fell in love with her. He proposed, was accepted and arrangements for the wedding were made. Then Maria, the elder sister, was involved in a serious scandal. Francis asked Elizabeth to break acquaintance with her, but Elizabeth had now fallen in love with, and later married, Colonel Campbell, future Duke of Argyll, and the engagement was broken off. So Elizabeth Gunning married two dukes and jilted a third.

Disappointed in love, Francis turned to the management of his estates and, in 1757, came to Worsley and its coal mines.

It happened that this same year the St Helens Canal had been opened, the first true canal in Britain since Roman times. Henry Berry, dock engineer at Liverpool, had been commissioned by that city's common council in 1754 to survey and widen the Sankey brook from St Helens to the river Mersey. The object was to facilitate the transportation of coal and reduce its cost. The Enabling Act passed by Parliament in 1755 permitted new cuts to be made to straighten the brook. Berry went much further than this and joined the new cuts together making an artificial navigation falling through twelve locks to the river Mersey. The resulting navigation operated commercially until 1959.

JOHN GILBERT

The immediate consequences for the Duke of Bridgewater

were most serious. Already flooding at his Worsley mines made coal-mining expensive and now this navigation undercut the cost of his coal in Liverpool. The Duke's agent at Worsley was John Gilbert. His elder brother, Thomas, born in 1720, was chief legal agent to the Bridgewater estates and land agent to Earl Gower of Trentham. The brothers were sons of Thomas Gilbert, squire of Cotton Hall, now Cotton College, near Alton, Staffordshire. While Thomas had full legal training, John, at the age of thirteen, was apprenticed to Matthew Boulton, a prosperous manufacturer of jewellery in Birmingham. There he became great friends with Boulton's son, also Matthew, later to become famous as the co-founder, with James Watt, of the world-famous firm of Boulton and Watt, steam engine manufacturers.

In 1742 Thomas Gilbert, the father, died and John took over the management of the Cotton Hall Estate. In 1757 he was superseded by his elder brother Thomas, and John moved to Worsley. So, in the same year as the St Helens Canal was opened, an enterprising agent arrived at Worsley, as did young Francis, third Duke of Bridgewater, determined to throw himself into the improvement of his estate to forget his unfortunate love affair. This young Duke also had first-hand knowledge of, and an abiding interest in, canals.

There were two major obstacles to making the Worsley coal mines profitable—flooding and transport. The normal way of draining the shallow mines of those days—men or horses drawing up a bucket—was totally inadequate. Another method, where the coal seam lay at a higher level than the country round about, was to drive a sough (or tunnel) from the mine to this lower ground. This had been done at Worsley, but badly, and was very costly to maintain. Transport at this time was by horse and cart (or packhorse) and was most expensive. There was the Mersey and Irwell Navigation, which, by use of rivers and six locks carried goods to a quay between Manchester and Salford and charged twelve shillings a ton in contrast to forty shillings per ton by wagon or packhorse. But this was subject to the vagaries of weather, floods, water shortage and silting up of the channel.

In 1737 Manchester businessmen associated with the Mersey and Irwell Navigation Co. had obtained an act to construct a navigable canal from near Worsley to the river Irwell at Barton.

There it was to join the Mersey and Irwell Navigation, but it was not constructed. To John Gilbert must go the credit of conceiving the idea of excavating a new sough to drain the Worsley mine. This would be at a lower level than the old one and constructed on a scale big enough to allow the loading of coal-barges inside the mine.

WORSLEY AND BRIDGEWATER CANALS PROJECTED

The sough would be extended in the form of a canal to Manchester and this would solve three problems—the drainage of the mine; the supply of water to work the canal; and the transport of the coal.

The young Duke, not only fascinated by canals but also saying that 'A navigation should always have coals at the heels of it', was so enthused by the idea that he decided not only to construct the Worsley Canal to Manchester but to extend it westwards to the river Mersey, at Runcorn, for Liverpool. He immediately went to Liverpool and for £4,200 purchased the land that would be needed for docks there. In March 1759 he obtained an act of Parliament to construct a canal from Worsley to Salford. In it, the Duke bound himself not to charge more than 2s 6d per ton for the carriage of coal from Worsley to Manchester and not to charge the inhabitants more than 4d per hundredweight of 120 lbs of coal. These charges were to apply for the next forty years, less than half the price asked at that time.

John Gilbert had done much of the spade work, but a prominent experienced engineer was required to carry out the plan. Who better than James Brindley, constructor of the nearby Clifton Colliery scheme, of so many dams, sluices, water and windmills and already employed by Earl Gower, one of the Duke's guardians, in surveying the Trent and Mersey, or Grand Trunk (so named because of the branches which were expected to spread from it) Canal?

On the 1st July 1759 Brindley arrived at Worsley, staying six days. He suggested that the proposed canal should terminate at Stretford and that there it could make a junction with a canal from Manchester to be built to the Trent and Mersey Canal that he had already surveyed. The Duke agreed, and Brindley surveyed the new route. This required a new act of Parliament, and Brindley, in his capacity as engineer to the canal, made the

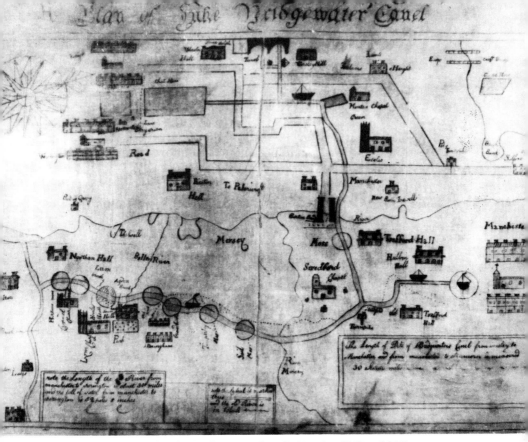

Brindley's 'Plan of Duke Bridgewater Canel'. Worsley Hall and Mill are at the top, Manchester and Trafford Hall are on the right, and Lymm church is on the left.

five-day journey to London on horseback to give evidence before the Parliamentary Committee concerned, and the act was passed early in 1760. Brindley had already started work under the powers of the old act to construct the canal into the mine at Worsley. At the same time he kept up with his work as a millwright and purchased a quarter share of the mineral-rich Turnhurst Estate, near Goldenhill, Stoke-on-Trent. The other shareholders were his brother, John Brindley, Hugh Henshall (afterwards his brother-in-law), John and Thomas Gilbert.

THE WORSLEY TO MANCHESTER CANAL

The new act being obtained, work proceeded apace. It had been decided that the canal should be on one level and the original plan, that of constructing locks to lower the canal to the river Irwell and raise it on the other side, was replaced by a plan to build an aqueduct at Barton. Although the Duke had seen such a structure when abroad, the idea was novel to England, so his friends expostulated with him and strongly advised him not to throw his money away. At Brindley's suggestion, an eminent engineer, thought to have been John Smeaton, was called in to give a second opinion and, to his dismay, declared against the project stating: 'I have often heard of castles in the air, but never saw where any of them were to be erected.'

The Duke was determined, but could the triumvirate of the Duke, Brindley and Gilbert carry out the project? The problems involved were not only technical: Dr John Aiken, in *A Description of the Country from Thirty to Forty Miles round Manchester* (1795), describes Brindley as being 'in appearance and manners as well as acquirements a mere peasant. Unlettered and rude of speech, it was easier for him to devise means for executing a design, than to communicate his ideas concerning it to others.' However, the scale of the job to be done at Worsley was so large that differences were ignored, although at times it required all the tact that the Duke could summon to keep the partnership going. On one occasion John Gilbert's stallion broke into the paddock of Brindley's mare and got her in foal. When Brindley swore that Gilbert had done it on purpose a furious row developed which had to be resolved by the Duke.

The aqueduct was something that no one in England had ever attempted before and was, for those days, of enormous size. The aqueduct was built, but on the day of its opening, when the water was let in, one of the arches showed signs of giving way. Brindley, exhausted by weeks of overwork, was overcome with anxiety and retired to bed. John Gilbert, realising that there was too much weight in the arch, removed the clay, laid straw on the stone-work and layers of freshly puddled clay. There was no further trouble and on 17th July 1761 barges of coal from the Duke's collieries at Worsley were crossing it on their journey to Manchester.

The Barton Aqueduct was a spectacle. People flocked to see boats sailing high above the boats on the river Irwell. It was about 200 yards long, 12 yards wide and carried by a stone bridge of three arches at a height of 39 feet above the river.

*Above: The Barton Aqueduct as featured in the 'Gentleman's Magazine',
1766. People flocked to see this 'wonder of the age'. Below: The
entrance to the canal tunnel at Worsley.*

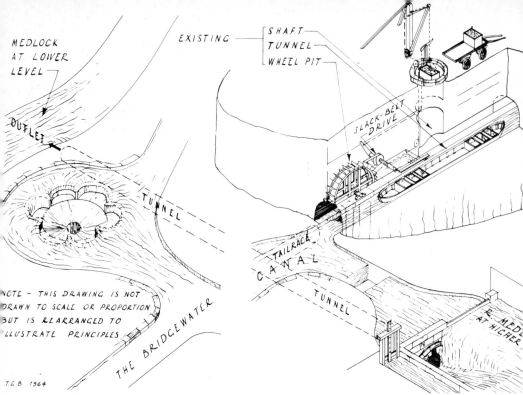

The centre arch had a span of 63 feet. In 1894 it was replaced by a swing-tank when the Manchester Ship Canal was built.

Although this was the major wonder, there were others. The Stretford embankment was 900 yards long. A writer in the *St. James' Chronicle* of 30th September 1763 described the ventilation of the Worsley mine as follows:

'At the mouth of the cavern . . is a water bellows, being the body of a tree forming a hollow cylinder standing upright. Upon this a wooden basin is fixed in the form of a funnel, which receives a current of water from the higher ground. This water falls into the cylinder, and issues out at the bottom of it but at the same time carries a quantity of air with it, which is received into the innermost recesses of the coal-pits where is issues out as from a pair of bellows, and rarifies the body of

24

thick air which would otherwise prevent the workmen from subsisting on the spot where the coals are dug.'

Brindley later installed a steam engine to pump out the reaches of the mine below the level of the canal. It is reputed that he built this engine for £150, against the usual price of £500. It is recorded that the success of the canal into the mines at Worsley led to the construction, in the late 1770s, of the Speedwell mine, near Castleton in Derbyshire, where the intention was to use the canal to carry lead-ore. After an expenditure of £14,000 the tunnel reached the 'Bottomless Pit', where a stream plunges into an apparent void. The promoters lost all their money, but today visitors can travel along the underground canal to visit the 'Bottomless Pit' and the magnificent cascade.

To reduce the danger from flooding when the canal banks burst, as they did in the early days, Brindley sank wooden gates into the bed of the canal. The pressure of any escaping water released catches and counterweights raised the gates to seal the breach in the canal.

At Castlefield, Manchester, the canal joined the river Medlock. Brindley adopted the principal of never allowing river or brook to mix with a canal except for the purpose of supply and to control the river Medlock a barrier was put across with a paddle, or shutter, on one side that could be raised or lowered to regulate the water. The river itself was taken under the canal by a tunnel. The flow of water drove a water-wheel that operated a hoist to lift the coal from the boats to street level. The final cost of the construction of the Worsley Canal was 1,000 guineas per mile.

All the work was financed by the Duke of Bridgewater who reduced his personal expenditure to £400 per annum. Even so, he was compelled to borrow where he could, mortgaging estates and selling land where permissible while many times the whole enterprise narrowly escaped financial ruin.

BRINDLEY IN LONDON

The Worsley section being a complete success, the Duke, Brindley and John Gilbert turned their attention to the westward extension across Cheshire to the river Mersey and Liverpool. For this, a fresh act of Parliament was required and from August to November 1761 Brindley was engaged in obtaining this act. His remuneration was 7s 6d per day plus board and lodging.

In January 1762 he was in London to assist in the passage of the bill through Parliament. He spent money on rigging himself out with a new outfit: 'New briches £1-1s-8d, Cloth coat and wast(coat) of broad cloth £2-2s-0d, for new shoes 0-6s-0d, at the play 0-9s-0d'. Gilbert apparently persuaded Brindley to see Garrick in the play *Richard III* and, never having been to that kind of entertainment before, the excitement was so great and so disturbed his ideas that he was unfit for business for several days.

Before the Parliamentary Committee on the bill, when asked to explain the buildings of aqueducts and how a canal would be made watertight, he gave an 'ocular demonstration'. He bought a large cheese which he cut in halves, saying that each half represented an arch of the aqueduct, the canal lying in a trough across them. He then made a trough out of sand and clay and poured water into it which ran out. He then 'puddled' the mixture (i.e. mixed them together with water), remade the trough, poured in water and none leaked away. 'Puddling' clay to make canals watertight was not the only discovery that Brindley made. He had the ability to cope with all problems, however serious, and is credited with the design and execution of many devices including the control of breaches in canals by automatic gates, hopper-barges, the giant caisson for advancing embankments and also the patent boiler, to name just a few. When faced with an obtuse problem he would retire to bed to think it over, staying there for as long as three days, and emerging with the problem solved. Calculations were all performed in his head, the working being written down only as parts of a project were completed.

Asked to explain the working of a lock before a committee of the House of Lords he pulled a piece of chalk from his pocket and drew a diagram on the floor of the room. Their lordships understood from his drawing and explanation how locks operated.

On 5th March 1762 the bill was passed. Brindley recorded it as follows:

'ad a grate Division of   127 fort Duk
                           98 nos
                          ____

for te Duke   29 Me Jorete'

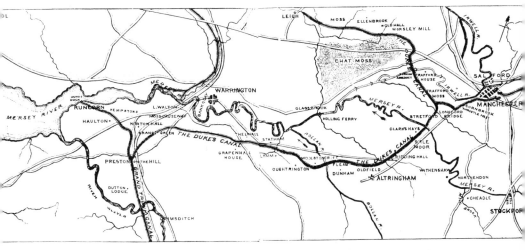

The Bridgewater Canal from Worsley to Manchester and Runcorn.

CONSTRUCTION OF THE MAIN BRIDGEWATER CANAL

The construction of the Bridgewater Canal began. As with the Worsley Canal, it was intended to keep it on one level, although a flight of locks was to be built to drop the canal to the level of the river Mersey at Runcorn.

The difficulties were enormous. An aqueduct with a single span of seventy feet was built to carry the canal across the Mersey at Stretford while Sale Moor was crossed by constructing a three-sided casing of wood, open at the side where the canal embankment was being built. When the embankment reached the correct height, the casing was moved on and the filling process repeated.

A massive embankment was raised to carry the canal across the valley of the river Bollin. A portion of this collapsed in August 1971 and is the only known instance of one of Brindley's structures giving way. This was over two hundred years after its construction. This work was done during 1767 and Brindley had already been seconded to engineer the Trent and Mersey (Grand Trunk) Canal. However, he was still on the Duke's payroll as consultant-engineer.

As the canal was extended it was used to carry as much as

possible of the materials and equipment needed for its construction. Perhaps the most interesting transporting device was a 'hopper' carried between two hulls. The hopper was loaded with sand, clay or other materials required and towed to the spot where needed. The bolts were then withdrawn and trapdoors opened so that the contents fell where required, a box or caisson protecting the place from flooding by the canal already constructed. There was a floating blacksmith's forge, a mason's boat, a carpenter's boat and even a floating chapel.

However, work on the Bridgewater Canal was held up because the original line had been altered so that instead of making its own way direct to the Mersey, it was to be joined at Preston Brook by the proposed Trent and Mersey Canal. Unfortunately this entailed cutting through the land of Sir Richard Brooks at Norton Priory. Sir Richard opposed this intrusion and persuaded neighbouring landlords to do likewise. Due to this opposition the Bridgewater Canal, providing a through waterway route between Manchester and Liverpool, was not completed until 1776.

The Duke's charge was six shillings per ton against twelve shillings by river and forty shillings by land carriage, between Manchester and Liverpool. By the time the canal was opened the Duke had acquired a debt of some £3 million at present-day rates.

In 1769 a passenger-boat service was introduced, beginning with a service between Worsley, Manchester and Lymm, near Warrington, which was later extended to Liverpool. The fare was one penny per mile, but Elisa Meteyard records Josiah Wedgwood as having travelled to Worsley and writing: 'Between Warrington and Manchester, the Duke has set up two passenger boats, one at one shilling each. The other divided into 3 rooms, 2s 6d for best, 10d and 12d, the pleasantest and cheapest mode of travel you can conceive.'

Each boat was drawn by two or three fast horses and equipped with a sharp sword at the prow to cut the tow-rope of any craft that failed to get out of the way. The Duke of Bridgewater had a handsome gondola after the fashion of Venice for his own use.

The income from the whole enterprise—Worsley, Manchester, Runcorn and Liverpool—reached £80,000 per annum. James Brindley's wage whilst engaged on the work was 7s 0d per day!

The Grand Cross

THE TRENT AND MERSEY (GRAND TRUNK) CANAL

In 1717 a Dr Thomas Congrave of Wolverhampton had published a pamphlet entitled *A Scheme and Proposal for making navigable communication between the Rivers of Trent and Severn in the County of Stafford.* In 1755 certain merchants of Liverpool had the line for a prospective canal surveyed. This was to proceed by Chester to Stafford, Derby and Nottingham but it did not go forward.

James Brindley's 'Grand Cross' scheme was to join the Mersey to the Thames by means of a canal and a second canal would join the Trent to the Severn. A 'Grand Cross' would thus be formed, linking the four great ports of London, Liverpool, Bristol and Hull. Further branches were planned to Manchester, Birmingham, Coventry and Derby.

Brindley had already done a survey for a canal in 1758 for Earl Gower and Lord Anson but its high cost, coupled with doubts as to its feasibility, caused its sponsors to abandon it. The success of the Duke of Bridgewater's canal from Worsley to Manchester revived interest. Furthermore, the extension of that canal to the river Mersey had been realigned to make a junction with the proposed Grand Trunk Canal. This would give the Bridgewater Canal access to the Potteries, Hull and, eventually, London and Bristol and give the Grand Trunk access to Manchester and Liverpool. The Duke of Bridgewater accordingly threw his whole weight behind the revived scheme.

Brindley's 'hopper' boats.

Another worthy protagonist now entered the scene—Josiah Wedgwood. He was already acquainted with Brindley and was fully aware of his abilities and success. Josiah Wedgwood's origins were almost as humble as Brindley's. Youngest of a family of thirteen, his father died when Josiah was a young boy and his grandfather and uncle were little more than cottage potters. Despite this, and a right leg amputated as a result of smallpox, he had begun to transform the pottery industry, improving its products immeasurably and introducing methods of working that had both cheapened and increased production.

Unfortunately, the only methods of transporting his products to his customers were by pack-man, horse wagon or packhorse (the latter costing 1s 0d per ton mile), all of which were very slow and causing great waste through breakage. The best wares needed flint from south-east England and china clay from Cornwall and Devon. Boats carried flints up the Trent to Wilden Ferry and clay up the river Weaver to Winsford, or up the Severn to Bridgnorth and Bewdley, and thence by packhorse or wagon. All produce was carried in the same costly way.

To Josiah Wedgwood, transport by canal offered immense strategic advantages. It would ease conveyance to his English customers and increase his considerable business with Europe and America. If the Grand Cross scheme came about, the Potteries would have waterway routes to Manchester, Liverpool, Hull, Bristol and London and prospects for manufacture and trade would expand beyond belief.

BEGINNING OF THE TRENT AND MERSEY CANAL COMPANY

The first public meeting was held at Wolseley Bridge, Staffordshire, on 30th December 1765. Earl Gower of Trentham occupied the chair. Lord Grey and Mr Bagot, MPs for the county, Mr Anson, MP for Lichfield, Thomas Gilbert, agent to Earl Gower and MP for Newcastle, Staffordshire Josiah Wedgwood and other influential gentlemen were present.

Josiah Wedgwood, when reporting on the meeting, said: 'Brindley was called upon to state his plans, brought them forward with such extraordinary lucidity of detail as to make them clear to the dullest intellect present'. The plans were accepted and it was determined that steps should be taken to put a bill before the next session of Parliament. Wedgwood

Josiah Wedgwood FRS, 1730-95, from the portrait by Sir Joshua Reynolds. Wedgwood championed Brindley's scheme for a 'Grand Cross' of canals connecting Manchester, Liverpool, Hull, Bristol and London.

promised one thousand pounds towards preliminary expenses and to subscribe for a large number of shares besides. The promoters wished to call the undertaking 'The Canal from the Trent to the Mersey'. Brindley urged that it should be called the Grand Trunk Canal, as he judged that it would be the main artery from which other canals would branch.

The decision to promote the bill caused much rejoicing in the Potteries and the healths of all the gentlemen concerned were drunk round a huge bonfire in Burslem.

MARRIAGE TO ANNE HENSHALL

Meanwhile, an event of a more personal nature to James Brindley had taken place—his marriage to Anne Henshall on 8th December 1765.

In 1762 Brindley had become associated with John Henshall, a land surveyor of Newchapel, near Tunstall, Staffordshire. Henshall had a young daughter named Anne, to whom Brindley took a fancy. He always ensured that he had gingerbread in his pocket for the girl when he visited her father. The liking ripened into affection and when Anne reached the age of nineteen Brindley, now forty-nine years of age, proposed, was accepted and they married. As it happened, Turnhurst Hall, Newchapel, became vacant, so the newly-weds moved in, it being most convenient for Brindley's workshops at Burslem, the Goldenhill Colliery and the prospective construction of the Grand Trunk Canal.

Anne proved a most capable help-meet and took over most of the writing for her ill-lettered husband. Her brother, Hugh Henshall, became one of Brindley's assistants and later completed the Trent and Mersey and Chesterfield canals, eventually becoming general manager of the Trent and Mersey Canal Company. James Brindley was extremely competent in the selection and training of his assistants, many of whom became first-class engineers in their own rights. Robert Whitworth was the most successful of these. He worked on the Birmingham and Coventry canals and partnered his brother to construct most of the Leeds and Liverpool Canal, later becoming engineer of the Forth and Clyde Canal. Others include Samuel Simcock (probably married to Brindley's sister, Esther) who assisted Brindley on the Staffordshire and Worcestershire, and Birmingham canals, and took over the

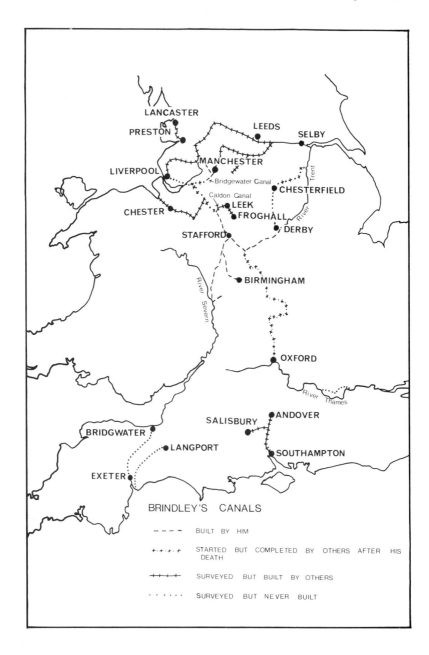

BRINDLEY'S CANALS

- - - -   BUILT BY HIM

+·+·+   STARTED BUT COMPLETED BY OTHERS AFTER HIS
         DEATH

+++++   SURVEYED BUT BUILT BY OTHERS

· · · · · ·   SURVEYED BUT NEVER BUILT

A view of the former Wedgwood factory alongside the Trent and Mersey Canal at Etruria.

construction of the Oxford Canal; Thomas Dadford, who played a great part in the building of the Staffordshire and Worcestershire Canal; and Samuel Weston, who worked on the Oxford Canal and also constructed the Chester Canal.

RIVAL SCHEMES

There were rival schemes to Brindley's Grand Trunk Canal. One was from the river Weaver to the Trent, which would have entailed a long haul round Runcorn and the Mersey to reach Manchester and would not connect with the Bridgewater Canal, so the Duke of Bridgewater was against it. Another proposal was a canal from the river Dee near Chester to Stoke, but the objections to the river Weaver scheme applied to this with even greater force.

The contest in Parliament between the river Weaver faction

and the supporters of the Grand Trunk Canal was a fierce one, with Brindley as chief parliamentary witness for the latter. The bill was not passed until 3rd May 1766 and the 'Company of Proprietors of the Navigation from the Trent to the Mersey' was then set up. Among the Committee of Management were John Brindley (the engineer's brother), Matthew Boulton (later of Boulton and Watt, the famous steam engine builders) and Josiah Wedgwood. The latter was appointed Treasurer and granted himself no salary whatsoever; James Brindley was Surveyor-General at £200 per annum and Hugh Henshall became Clerk of Works at £150 per annum.

On 26th July 1766 Josiah Wedgwood cut the first sod of the canal at Brownhills near Tunstall. Many local personages followed suit. Brindley was present and was congratulated on all sides. Later, a sheep was roasted whole in Burslem market place and shared among the poor people. A bonfire was lit before Wedgwood's home and there was general rejoicing.

In the following year Wedgwood purchased the Ridgehouse estates adjoining the line of the canal and proceeded to move his entire manufactory there. He named the new works 'Etruria' after the decorated pottery discovered in the excavations at Pompeii and thought to be the work of the Etruscans. Wedgwood's works in the early years were driven by an extraordinary windmill devised by Dr Erasmus Darwin. In 1939 a new works, employing more than two thousand people, was built at Barlaston, about five miles away and the old one closed down.

After the celebrations at Burslem work on the canal started. Brindley had predicted that the whole canal would be finished by the end of 1772 but this was not to be owing to delays with the tunnel through Harecastle Hill, west of Stoke-on-Trent.

HARECASTLE TUNNEL

The tunnel through a variety of difficult rocks and quicksands was to be some 2,880 yards long, 9 feet wide and 12 feet high. It was to be the first ever tunnel built solely for transport purposes. Much tunnelling had been done before in mines in pursuit of coal or ores, but whereas these tunnels could rise or fall or twist in following the seams the Harecastle Tunnel, being a canal tunnel, had to be dead level and straight. Brindley had already proved at Clifton that he could engineer a tunnel, but that one was 600 yards long, about six feet wide and near to the surface.

One may wonder why Brindley decided to go through the hill, for British Rail engineers, when they came to electrify the railway line in 1965, found a way round needing only a short tunnel. Brindley had a very good eye for country and must have been aware of this route. One reason may be that the Harecastle section was at the summit of the canal. Going round the hill would have entailed a series of locks up one side and down the other, needing an abundant supply of water which was not available. Perhaps the fact that clinched the matter was the nearness of Goldenhill colliery to Harecastle Hill. If a tunnel were constructed, side canals could be driven into the seams of the mine and, as at Worsley, coal could be loaded straight from the mine into the canal boats. In the event this was done. It is recorded that the tunnel connecting Goldenhill colliery with Harecastle Tunnel was one and a half miles long.

When in 1827 Thomas Telford eased the bottle-neck on the Trent and Mersey Canal caused by Brindley's tunnel he had concluded that the decision to go through Harecastle Hill was the correct one, and constructed his relief tunnel alongside Brindley's original one. In 1848 the North Staffordshire Railway line from Macclesfield to Norton Bridge was put through Harecastle Hill on the same line but at a slightly higher level. Neither water nor access to coal seams nor the need to keep to one level were a consideration. Yet the decision was made to go through and, despite the tremendous advances in civil engineering since Brindley's day, it still proved a most difficult undertaking. Eventually Irish 'navvies' (derived from tough navigation labourers) were procured to finish the job. Even British Rail's much shorter new tunnel, 250 yards, was only constructed with great difficulty, the ground above being of fractured shale.

When Brindley revealed his plan to go through Harecastle Hill it was greeted with great derision, and people confidently predicted that it would be another castle in the air, being impossible to construct. Yet the previous 'castle', Barton Aqueduct, had refuted all criticism.

Work commenced in July 1766. A line was surveyed over the hill, fifteen intermediate shafts were dug down to the proposed level of the canal and work started at each end, so thirty-two

Above: A somewhat fanciful representation of Brindley's 2,880 yard tunnel through Harecastle Hill on the Trent and Mersey Canal.
Below: The entrances to Brindley's Harecastle tunnel (1777) (right) and Thomas Telford's relief tunnel (1827) alongside it.

faces were being worked at once. Spoil excavated was raised by horse-gin. The stone was so hard that it was almost impossible to penetrate it and the contractors for Telford's tunnel stated that in Harecastle Hill they found the hardest rock in their whole experience. Most unfortunate was the presence of water, essential for the completed canal, but a great impediment during construction.

At first, pumps operated by windmill, horse or man kept the water in check, but eventually the onrush was too great and work stopped until Brindley could erect a pump driven by a steam engine. Then, where the tunnel passed through the coal measures, fire-damp, a dangerous explosive gas, was met. This danger Brindley removed by placing stoves at the bottom of the shafts, so that the heat rising from them drew down fresh air into the workings. The tunnel was lined and arched with brick.

In September 1767 a contemporary of Brindley wrote: 'Gentlemen come to view our eighth wonder of the world, the subterraneous navigation, which is cutting by the great Mr Brindley, who handles rock as easily as you would plum pies, and makes the four elements subservient to his will. He is as plain a looking man as one of the boors of the Peake, or one of his own carters; but when he speaks, all ears listen, and every mind is filled with wonder, at the things he pronounces to be practicable. He has cut a mile through bogs, which he binds up, embanking them with stones which he gets out of other parts of the navigation, besides a quarter of a mile into the hill Yelden; on the side of which he has a pump, which is worked by water, and a stove, the fire of which sucks through a pipe the damps that would annoy the men, who are cutting towards the centre of the hill. The clay he cuts out serves for bricks, to arch the subterraneous part, which we heartily wish to see finished to Wilden Ferry, when we shall be able to send coal and pots to London, and to different parts of the globe.'

After Brindley's death in 1772 the work went on under Hugh Henshall, his brother-in-law, and was finished in May 1777. Other tunnels were Armitage (now opened out), 130 yards; Barnton, 560 yards; Saltersford, 350 yards; and Preston on the Hill (near the junction with the Bridgewater Canal) 1,241 yards. None of the tunnels had towing paths, boats being propelled by the boatmen lying on their backs and 'legging' the boats through. The reward for legging a narrow boat through

Harecastle Tunnel, almost one and three quarter miles, was 1s 6d.

OTHER WORKS

In addition, the Grand Trunk (Trent and Mersey) Canal had 76 locks, 160 aqueducts, 213 road bridges, and comprised a total length of 93 miles from Preston Brook junction to Wilden Ferry, where it joined the navigable river Trent.

The longest aqueduct, twelve arches, carried the canal over the river Dove. In the embankment are a further eleven aqueducts, so the crossing of the Dove by itself was a major feat of civil engineering. Brindley built his major aqueducts by first building half the structure on dry land, then excavating a channel to divert the river under the new structure. This enabled the other half to be built on dry land and when complete, the river was released so that it could flow through both old and new channels. Thus Brindley's methods allowed building on dry land and created extra space for flooding. They are very broad and sturdy structures as they had to support not

The aqueduct which Brindley built to take the Trent and Mersey Canal over the river Dove near Clay Mills, Staffordshire.

only the weight of the water, but the mass of clay and earth to contain it.

The word 'lock' is believed to derive from the Anglo-Saxon *loc,* an enclosure. 'Flash' locks, a comparatively old invention, were a means of impounding a river, usually by means of a gate, thus raising the level of the river so that boats could pass. The pound lock, with a single gate at the top and a double, mitred gate at the bottom, although a much later invention, was already in use before Brindley's time. (There were ten on the St Helens Canal). The size of the standard lock was fixed at 74 feet 9 inches long and 7 feet wide at a meeting of canal companies at Lichfield on 15th December 1769. The lock at Compton on the Staffordshire and Worcestershire Canal was the first of Brindley's locks to be completed.

When the Trent and Mersey Canal Act was passed on 14th May 1766, another act was passed authorising the Staffordshire and Worcestershire Canal. This was to leave the Trent and Mersey Canal at Great Haywood, cross the river Trent by a four-arch aqueduct, then traverse fairly easy country by Wolverhampton and Kidderminster to join the river Severn at Stourport.

This canal was forty-six miles long and needed forty-three locks as well as road bridges, and was opened throughout for traffic by May 1772. As the stretch of the Trent and Mersey Canal from Wilden Ferry on the Trent to Stoke was also open by this time, Brindley had the satisfaction of seeing two arms of his great Grand Cross scheme completed, linking the Potteries with the major ports of Bristol and Hull.

COVENTRY AND OXFORD CANALS

The next part of the Grand Cross scheme was to link the Trent and Mersey Canal with the river Thames and London by means of a canal from Fradley Junction near Lichfield, Staffordshire, to the Thames at Oxford. Brindley surveyed the route and saw the necessary act through Parliament, which gave its assent in January 1768. For the purpose of constructing the canal two companies were set up, the Coventry Canal Co, and the Oxford Canal Co. The Coventry Canal was to run from Fradley Junction to Coventry; at Longford, thirty-four miles from Fradley Junction, the Oxford Canal (authorised in 1769) was to go off to the Thames at Oxford.

Brindley's theodolite (or level) and oat-cake spoon (owner Mrs A. H. Ackroyd, Chichester). The level is on display at the James Brindley Museum, Leek.

The Coventry Canal Navigation Co held its first meeting in Coventry on 19th February 1769. Half the management were aldermen or councillors of the City of Coventry; Brindley was appointed Engineer and Surveyor, salary £250 per annum, with Joseph Parker as Clerk of Works, £150 per annum. Work started with some vigour, but at a meeting of the company held on 12th September 1769 Brindley was dismissed and Parker threatened with dismissal. It appears that Brindley's standard of construction was too expensive and so, having more than enough work on his hands, Brindley severed connection with this canal.

Joseph Parker was sacked in 1770 but construction continued until 1771 when it reached Atherstone, 16½ miles. At this point the company ran out of money and work did not restart until 1788, seventeen years later.

The Oxford Canal Company held its first meeting in May 1769 and appointed Brindley Engineer and Surveyor at £200 per annum, with Samuel Simcock as his assistant. According to the Parliamentary plan, the length was to be eighty-two miles. The committee of the company had the Vice-Chancellor of the

University as Chairman, and the members were the heads of the various colleges, who were anxious to get construction going. In 1769 they complained that Brindley had failed to give an estimate, and nagged to such good effect that a year later Brindley sent his resignation. This brought them to their senses for they sent a letter of apology, desiring his presence at their next meeting, and Brindley resumed his responsibilities. On his death in 1772 Samuel Simcock took over. The company ran into financial difficulties and Banbury was not reached until 1779, and the Thames not until 1793. As first constructed the canal was ninety-one miles long and this completed the Grand Cross, but major branches were started in Brindley's time.

OTHER CANALS

In February 1768 an act was obtained for a canal to Birmingham. This was to leave the Staffordshire and Worcestershire Canal at Aldersley Junction and pass through Wolverhampton and Smethwick to Birmingham, a distance of twenty-four miles. Brindley was appointed Engineer and Surveyor at £200 per annum and among the promoters of this canal were Matthew Boulton and Josiah Wedgwood. The canal was completed in September 1772, a week before Brindley died.

Another canal engineered by Brindley and opened before he died was the Droitwich Canal. This was started in 1768 and completed in 1771, Brindley being paid £60 per annum. Although only six miles long, it opened up a considerable trade in coal and salt between Droitwich and the river Severn. It descended from Droitwich to the river at Hawford by means of eight locks and was a very worthwhile canal.

In 1769 construction of a canal from Chesterfield, Derbyshire, to the Trent, forty-six miles away, was authorised. Work started in 1771 at Norwood, where a tunnel 2,850 yards long had to be cut, and Brindley expected to finish the whole canal in 1776. The work was continued after Brindley's death by Hugh Henshall and completed in 1777. Carrying coal, lime and lead from mineral-rich Derbyshire, it became a very prosperous concern.

The original survey for the Leeds and Liverpool Canal, 127 miles, was not performed by Brindley and proved impracticable. Brindley was summoned in July 1768 and was asked to make a new survey. Accompanied by his assistant, Robert Whitworth, John Longbottom, Resident Engineer, and John Hustler, prospective manager, this was done. The new survey was accepted, an act of Parliament obtained in July 1769, and Brindley was offered the post of Engineer but declined owing to pressure of work. Robert Whitworth and his brother started the construction, but it was so long and difficult that they did not live to see its completion in 1816.

Brindley surveyed the Lancaster Canal, which was intended to connect the Leeds and Liverpool Canal with Preston, Lancaster and Kendal, but it was resurveyed and built by John Rennie. Brindley also surveyed the canal to connect Bradford with Leeds and Liverpool, and did some work on the Calder and Hebble Navigation. In order to connect this with the Bridgewater Canal he surveyed the Rochdale Canal, thirty-three miles long, but it was not started during his lifetime. In the same category are the Chester Canal; the Huddersfield Broad Canal; the Leeds and Selby Canal; the Forth and Clyde Canal; the Andover Canal; the Salisbury and Southampton Canal; the Sheffield and South Yorkshire Navigation; a canal to Shrewsbury; the Stockton and Darlington Canal; to Swarkestone on the Trent and Mersey Canal; to Derby and Chesterfield; Runcorn to Liverpool, including an aqueduct over the tidal river Mersey 460 yards long; the Stockport Canal; a canal from the Bristol Channel to Exeter; one from Langport to Exmouth in Devon; a canal alongside the Thames from Sonning to Mortlake; and also proposals to improve the navigation of the Thames itself.

THE CALDON CANAL AND FINAL ILLNESS

Josiah Wedgwood and the management of the Trent and Mersey Canal Company decided to construct a branch canal from the summit at Etruria, Stoke-on-Trent, to Froghall in the valley of the river Churnet. The area was rich in coal and iron ore, but the main attraction was the limestone at Caldon Low.

Brindley surveyed the route and in September 1772 had reached Froghall. He got soaked to the skin, caught a chill, was taken to an inn in the village of Ipstones nearby and put into a damp bed. He became seriously ill and was taken to his home at Turnhurst. The eminent scientist and physician Dr Erasmus Darwin, friend of Josiah Wedgwood, the grandfather of Charles

Froghall Wharf, Caldon Canal, in its heyday.

Darwin, author of *The Origin of the Species,* was called in. He diagnosed the malady that had troubled Brindley for several years as diabetes.

It was now too late, the patient was beyond human aid. But not yet beyond his affairs, for even on his death bed some people in difficulty over constructing a canal demanded audience and advice. It was granted and they explained that they couldn't get their canal to hold water. 'Then puddle it,' said Brindley. When they explained that they had already done so he retorted: 'Then puddle it again and again,' and with that they had to be satisfied.

On 26th September 1772 Wedgwood wrote to his partner Thomas Bentley: 'Poor Mr. Brindley has nearly finished his course in this world. He says he must leave us, and indeed I do not expect to find him alive in the morning. His disorder, I think I told you, is a diabetes, and this malady he has had upon him for seven years past most probably, which occasioned his constant fever and thirst, though I believe no one of his doctors found it out till Dr Darwin discovered it in the present illness, which, I fear, will deprive us of a valuable friend, and the world of one of the great Geniuses who seldom live to see justice done to their singular abilities, but must trust to future ages for that tribute of praise and fair fame they so greatly merit from their fellow mortals.'

On 28th September 1772 Wedgwood wrote again: 'I told you in my last letter that Mr Brindley was extremely ill, and I have the grief to tell you that he is now no more. He died on the 27th inst. about 12 at noon, after giving him something to wet his mouth, he said, "It's enough, I shall need no more", and shut his eyes, never more to open.'

He left a young widow, Anne, and two daughters. Anne married Robert Williamson in 1775 and had seven children. She died in 1799.

Of Brindley's two daughters, Susannah married John Bettington in 1795 and they emigrated to Australia, had children and lived at Brindley's Plains, Tasmania. Anne, the other daughter, died on the voyage home from Sydney, Australia, in 1838.

James Brindley was buried in the churchyard of St James at Newchapel, Staffs, on 30th September 1772. The church was rebuilt in 1880 as a memorial to the first great civil engineer.

Brindley's burial place at Newchapel, Staffordshire.

THE PRINCIPAL EVENTS OF BRINDLEY'S LIFE

1716   James Brindley born at Tunstead, Derbyshire.
1726   Moves with family to farm at Leek as labourer.
1727   *Accession of George II.*
1733   Apprenticed to Abraham Bennett near Macclesfield.
1735   First identified as excellent workman.
1737   Completes machinery of paper-mill for Bennett.
1742   Starts in business as millwright in Leek.
1745   *Jacobite Rebellion; highlanders pass through Leek twice.*
1750   Opens workshop at Burslem.
1752   Builds Leek Mill; starts Clifton Hydraulic Power Scheme.
1756   Visits Bedworth, Birmingham and Wolverhampton to see steam engines; builds steam engine at Little Fenton.
1757   *Thomas Telford born.*
1758   Overhauls pumps for Earl Gower; windmill for grinding flints for Josiah and T. Wedgwood; patents steam engine boiler; survey for Grand Trunk Canal.
1759   Consulted by Duke of Bridgewater; commences Worsley to Manchester section of Bridgewater Canal.
1760   *Accession of George III.*
1761   Barton Aqueduct opens to traffic.
1762   Surveys for Chester Canal and Branch Canal to Stockport.
1763   Gives advice on Lower Avon Navigation improvements.
1764   Supervises construction of Bridgewater Canal.
1765   Marries Anne Henshall; appointed Engineer to Calder and Hebble Navigation.
1766   Work commences on Grand Trunk Canal.
1767   Surveys for Bradford Canal, Rochdale Canal and Stockton and Darlington Canal.
1768   Survey for Leeds and Liverpool Canal.
1769   Surveys for Leeds and Selby Canal and Oxford Canal.
1770   Prepares scheme for Thames navigation improvements.
1771   Chesterfield Canal commences,
1772   Survey for Lancaster Canal; taken ill at Froghall; dies on 27th September.

WHERE TO SEE BRINDLEY'S WORK

The Brindley Mill, a working water-driven mill restored as a memorial to Brindley, and containing the James Brindley Museum, may be seen at Leek in Staffordshire on the A523, Macclesfield to Leek road, about half a mile from the town centre. (See page 9.)

The scheme for draining Clifton Colliery is reached at the A666, Manchester to Bolton road, at Kearsley and A667 north of Kearsley for Ringley Fold. To see the Worsley (Bridgewater) Canal and the Delph take the A575 south of Exit 6 on the M62 motorway. At Great Haywood in Staffordshire (A51 between Stone and Rugeley) may be seen the junction of the Trent and Mersey and Staffs and Worcs Canals with locks, bridges and an aqueduct over the river Trent. At Alrewas, Staffordshire, may be seen a lock and level crossing of the Trent (A38 Burton to Lichfield, north of A513). The Dove aqueduct may be seen two miles north of Burton-on-Trent along the A38 from the old coach bridge over the river Dove. At Kidsgrove in Staffordshire is Harecastle tunnel (turn west in town centre along First Avenue, about 200 yards).

Tunstead, in Wormhill parish, near Buxton, has a plinth and plaque marking Brindley's birthplace. Wormhill decorates his memorial well and holds its annual fete on the last Saturday in August.

BIBLIOGRAPHY

Brindley at Wet Earth Colliery by A.G. Banks and R.B. Schofield (David and Charles).

James Brindley Engineer, 1716-1772 by C.T.G. Boucher (Goose and Son).

The Canal Duke by Hugh Malet (David and Charles).

A Description of the Country from thirty to forty miles round Manchester by John Aiken (John Stockdale, 1795).

History of the Ancient Parish of Leek by Hugh Sleigh (1862)

Life of Josiah Wedgwood by Eliza Meteyard (Hurst and Blackett, 1866).

Josiah Wedgwood by Richard Tames (Shire Publications Ltd, 1972).

Lives of the Engineers, Volume 1 by Samuel Smiles (David and Charles).

James Brindley — A Staffordshire Gazetteer (Staffordshire Planning Department).

INDEX

Page numbers in italic refer to illustrations